INTERFERON
PSALMS

— 33 psalms on the 99 names of God —

for Richard

Luke Davies

love from— Luke

ALLEN & UNWIN

Luke Davies

July 2021

First published in 2011

Australian Government

This project has been assisted by the Australian Government through the Australia Council, its arts funding and advisory board.

Allen & Unwin
Sydney, Melbourne, Auckland, London

83 Alexander Street
Crows Nest NSW 2065
Australia
Phone: (61 2) 8425 0100
Fax: (61 2) 9906 2218
Email: info@allenandunwin.com
Web: www.allenandunwin.com

Cataloguing-in-Publication details are available from the
National Library of Australia
www.trove.nla.gov.au

ISBN 978 1 74237 034 7

Typeset in 9/14 pt Centennial by Bookhouse

Printed and bound in Australia by Griffin Press

20 19 18 17 16 15 14 13

This life of yours is not a picture of the world. It is the world itself, and it is composed not of bone or dream or time but of worship.

CORMAC MCCARTHY, *Cities of the Plain*

I

1

Lift up our hearts.
Lift up our hearts. So then, lift up our hearts.

It is a flooded world: every available flood.
It is a flooded world: such floods of good.
Everything present, as it always was.
A flooded world; I'm sick with shallow corpuscle.

•

Skin turned to scale. Head peeled away. I am Reptile,
hear me roar.

On this earth I learned all about suffering. *Mutter, meine
Mutter,* the bandages stick to my skin.

All countries are equally evil, but some more evil than
others. Ditto for the sections of my body.

I would write nothing, from the perfect centre of a
monstrous place, O Holy One of Being. Nothing at all: that
was my plan. I had to gather the forces of my memory and

I had to trust my memory. But first I had to allow sheer bewilderment to flow through me.

•

She said: *I want to talk to you, at roughly four removes.*

But I am getting ahead of myself. First, bewilderment. Then the memory packs it in. Then bewilderment, protein-enriched. Then a long time later, the coast was clear, and I began to recollect. Which in no way diminished embarrassment and pain. O how the years passed.

Such grand sadness inside her, I mean me.

But I am getting ahead of myself.

•

In the centre of my life I lost its centre. *Touch his bone and flesh, and he will curse thee to thy face.*

The blade of my happiness broke at the hilt. I flailed, without balance, at air. A break at the hilt is a hard break to fix. Life in search of a blacksmith. Of bellows and tongs I knew little.

The rumpled magazines of waiting rooms.

The great lakes came and went. Winter rolled in for ten thousand years. I dreamed of heat, in lethargy.

All life became a leaving behind. There weren't alternative fullnesses.

There were stories written on calfskin, though I had no capacity for concentration. The lost would be found, on land, and by water.

It was never going to be a long love affair, but in my yielding I became a mystic.

I was staying the course. I felt the tightness.

•

Perhaps, O Witness, O Word, O Diadem of Beauty, perhaps the hummingbird would have been enough, its extravagant plausibility, its taste for weightlessness. I'd been a honeyeater too, myself, so weightless in the desert light. This was the arid time.

All the old men were dying or feeble and yet there were certain evenings when their ideas whirred like wings. Twenty years earlier, when I learned one could bow to the earth, or that there even was an earth, I was snapped out of my abstraction. I stopped hurting myself.

The monastery of sentience

Such moments of rupture. I cried that I had never seen the snow, having seen it now.

I was certainly in the place of licking wounds. Though not as a cat licks; I was certainly a bull.

But even a bull can be felled by flukeworm.

Eventually the universe will bo fclled.

Don't fret. A good interstice.

•

To have said *Go! Go!* to the bees. To have said *Disperse*.
To have understood a taxonomy of honey-gatherers.
To have seen the crane not as wing but as arabesque,
Inhabiting space in all but memory,
Punctuations of red its martyrdom,
This crane who forms these arabesques of light.

Wash me in the blood of mine enemies
And I shall be that I am.
We could bottle the rage and make money.

I emptied the spaces I tried to fill
But the unnerving stranger was always waiting.
I could not create enough bang and clang
To make him go away.
The sun set sparks of pure light
On the bullets of his gunbelt.
Walking down that long main street.
Saloon, oasis of my appetites.

•

There were no stop signs, no planets, nothing smaller than
galaxies. Just an endless plummeting away from her. This
proved fruitless and painful, so you open a door. You step
through. The birds feel the shockwaves. Their flight so
fervently runs rings around mine.

Then one day and for long after, words
Were all I had left. There was absolutely

Nothing else in the bereftness and now I was
A child once more; in any case, quite young.
Let it be, I said, to the jumble of words
Even as I rearranged them, and experiment
Returned. The specific always made me so
Rational. Also I was fighting the tide of many
Fools in the world—incredible, those numbers.
For a long time I had been too serious.
How to stop worrying about the architecture
Of the scansion of the rigging of the vessel
Of the bardic journey of the elders
And youngers alike was the lesson that
Awaited me. And all those fucking
Mouthfuls.
       I was exhausted.

How to elevate to first position
Honey Smacks or Froot Loops:
In any case this was the kind
Of lifestyle I was returning to—
But tenderly, so as not to give myself
Too hard a time of it.

Because of the desperation came the anxiety.
Out of the coffee the halitosis. The betrayal the triumph.
The bad boy the next bad boy:
Lined up for her as in a hall of mirrors.
Out of the wandering came the grocery list.
I always had a plan.

A decade passed like that.
Then the rains came and the soil softened.

I just let it fucking fly.

Chronology was never my finest hour
But only because I came to know time
Both inside and out so that
Reverence became a given;
And all, when all was good, was now.

But the mud leached up to my ankles and I went back
To looping in and out of the present. Damn!
Because I had for a while
That thing, that okay, that what, that *here*.
For God's sake, plant the flag.
Ain't nothing else'll grow
But the ensign of your selfhood,
That is to say, sovereignty.
So I saluted myself, feigning half-belief,
Which was abundantly more
Than what was truly necessary.

•

So foolish was I,
and ignorant:
I was as a beast
before thee.

Everywhere I went—and for years I went everywhere,
As if chased by myself—everywhere I went
I would always stock up at the supermarket
Because food became paying attention.
But the tins of tomatoes never travelled with me
To the next continent, the next supermarket.

Why leap ye,
ye high hills?
This is the hill of
the mercy seat.

A warning sign of any sort.
God no. Possibly I slept through it.
That would account for the shock as well as the awe.

The earthquake-addled desolation.
God yes. The jumble of masonry,
The concrete in its disarray. I'd picture coming home,
Across the welcome mat and through the open door.
I'd crawl into your open arms, for sure.

That's just not

Going to happen, I told myself. Pockets of realisation
Floating stateless and neutral like tiny planets. The bricks
All structureless and recently aflutter. Shock waves
Past their use-by date. The utter exhaustion
Of trying to maintain one's dignity amid one's pain.

I too became stateless and neutral.

The pleasure of your company. It was like being mugged.

For months, nothing is like the everything it should be.
The world is a little to the side of itself.

Navigational discomfort, the explorers called it.
A searing lock in the vertebrae, and in one's neck an
Ohmygodwhatthefuckisthat disaster of immobility.
For months, you clench the steering wheel.

The night sky was huge, but at any one time it was daylight
somewhere else: rendering the business calls impractical.
Time zones fattened out into the arhythmical haze of mere,
of sheer, loss.

I clung to my illuminations.

If every pen had a light in it my words would be of helium
and hydrogen, fused in a crucible, just like the textbooks
describe it. Or celestial globe.

•

None of this is happening.

•

I began to drift down to my death, like a ship heading ocean floorwards. On land, in my glory, I had been paramour and pirate rolled into one. Exceptionally talented. As I was a-walking down Paradise Street, a flash-looking packet I chanced for to meet. And now ten fathoms further, my cells were preparing for dispersal. It was uncanny, what sorrow looked like. I sensed in the darkness my cousins the squid. I was dying of course, like us all. I had lived on oxygen for so long, and now my lungs were panicked, then sad, and three atmospheres later I might as well have been tripping. Those were the last of my memories. The great kelp forests swaying. If I only had a sister, to hold her hand, then I would protect her, and forget about my fear, and we would walk under water, where the light shines.

It was a long slow world and time, by rivers and oceans.

2

The ice came back. If you sped up the centuries you could hear the morains screeching.

Retreated too. The forests grew again. We would have gone insane with the dripping of the leaves had we been around to hear it. But millions of years passed first. Psychiatry, cathedrals, they hadn't been invented. The rain leached minerals from the ground. Nothing could even take hold as future fossil.

The jungle overtook the temple of Ayesha. Vines strangled the masonry. The rocks were dislodged. We dreamed of enthusiastically savage sex. We were like Abbott and Costello, so frightened by the voodoo drums. But not thunder, never thunder. What is this thing that beats inside our chests, the early ones asked. They were soon to find out. The obsidian knife. Tied to the slab, I knew it was the last time I would see the sky. It seemed impossibly far away. Now I began to experience the fear without the anxiety, so this at last was a huge leap forward. In fact there was almost nothing here. Just light scattering through the molecules.

Deep calleth unto deep at the noise of thy water-spouts: all thy waves and thy billows are gone over me.

The sky impossibly far away. The solace leached from years of shame was that years were so short, once they were behind you. There was the hot blue and the cold blue: this was the cold blue. Snow flurries skittering on empty bridges. Slowly the salt and the antifreeze did their work. Eventually the bridge fell into the river, but this was only hearsay; I was long not there by then.

•

Four months pass

One day the rain fell for twenty thirsty minutes, and the sky cleared, and the mountains shone, and driving up Hillhurst, in the bubble of my car, I felt first flow and then connection. I not only wanted all bigger things to love me; I knew they did, in their own weird way. Nothing personal, the world said of its love.

My debt of gratitude, beginning to be paid, was stabbing me with now.

At least I got to bed a minute earlier each night, a minute at a time. It meant that in a decade I would find the perfect balance.

And eat my greens.

And all my blood would flow the way it should.

So slowly I figured this land where the living tumbled. But better late than never.

3

To walk so pointlessly backwards. Capacity for corrosion ever-present, ever-still. My shoulders locked up and I lost all touch with sleep. I had loved her. She had her own reasons. For some time I had no contact with my feelings, other than the distracted ones.

It was just another day of forward movement. I was aware of the blood rolling through me like treacle, but as for my breathing, I couldn't hear a thing.

I remembered my boon companion, a black-bottomed spoon. That was a journey and a half! My heart was grieved. I was pricked in my veins.

Gratitude as a by-product of memory.

Nature came back to reclaim pretty much everything. Even the buildings went soft. White cyclamen had bloomed in cracks, and slabs of street had buckled and lifted open.

Pavement made skewiff as if by giant hoe; by tiny seeds, insistent in their pushing, from below.

The feral geraniums didn't give up either.

Serenity as a
by-product of
prophecy

There is no indoor and outdoor. Only the flame trees and the thickets of hibiscus, only the drifts of mortar flaked to dust. Only house-shaped mounds of house-concealing bougainvillaea, and the houses deep inside long since strangled to collapse.

I wandered the fields of wild asparagus, through the prickly pear, in the searing heat. Whip snakes slithered at my feet.

All bees the one bee, I had once thought. My grandiose period. Now I saw the dead bees, sated on all that chlorine, in the swimming pool. It was each individual bee death that struck me; every circumstance in its time and place. I had become atomised rather than compartmentalised. It was a matter of viewing.

Cascades in my ears at night. That was the air-conditioning unit. Sirens were the birdsong of New York: there, even the dogs had given up barking.

•

I was never in one place at once. The dogs looked at me like strangers. But they took the time to look.

And yet the whole tale I was telling followed the rhythms of its necessity.

I anthropomorphised everything, even the scaffolders' ropes flapping bare and sunlit outside tenement kitchen windows: because everything was so lonely. Even the spindly basil in its planter box.

I ground myself into bone. Into ground bone, that is.

The old biologies will disappear beneath the sediments laid down.

4

The old geologies will disappear as the mountains erode, one pebble, one day, one freeze-thaw cycle at a time. Doesn't it all end up as limestone? I had had no idea how slow slow really was, since I was far more familiar with panic. In a Copenhagen summer, long ago, she had said, 'The day just passes so fast.' Myself, I was thinking, 'Life.'

The uplifts will pulverise to trace minerals, one day. The nutrients will nourish the new world.

I was preoccupied, emerging into the interglacial from the glaciation of my distress.

The present could turn so busy. I'd wake each morning, my blood mid-percolate, the day's hair-triggers of desire and chaos hovering as always as yet unborn, and some days it's all radio K-FUCK blaring inside me, so I turn down the dial on that one, O God of Hosts.

And the red-crowned cranes float down through the menace.

•

The world will be silent for thousands of years. Today, that made the loneliness even worse.

•

The panthers and jaguars came in from the jungle. They prowled the bollards where the ships once waited. All buckled concrete and thistles now. When the sluices have silted and the rain broken through, the rain-catch holes will disappear. The world will be silent for thousands of years.

I thought sadness was the route to forgetting, but months later anger was like a detour, and the smog settled on the city and made the dusk a glory, so I praised Yahweh, saying Holy One of Being, I am Yours and my Dreams are Yours. All that remained was to get to the gym. I did nothing for ages. I was trying to imitate the large-scale structures of being.

All my desire is before thee

But superclusters aside, I was generally part of the problem not the solution.

What else was there, but versions of sugar? There were other things, I know, I knew. But I was wandering in circles on an ice flow, for all I knew. A bag of sugar to keep me distracted and warm.

There were other things. But I couldn't be everywhere at once.

•

The wind passeth over it, and it is gone.

Purple asters split the pavement. Sun-bleak loneliness of forms. I revelled in the solitudes.

The petrochemical dodecahedrons which filled the air and rendered so pretty the dusks were pressed to the asphalt by the first rain in months. Thousands of years later they were well and truly absorbed into the soil. One might even say dispersed. (I had had unfinished business in other combinations of molecules. It all came out in the wash.)

My blood was crawling with messianic impropriety. I was a plasma-electric hybrid; it gave me more staying power through the galaxy of my auto-disdain. Or love, I forget which. Or loves.

My heart was hot within me. While I was musing, the fire burned.

It was a pleasure doing business with my doubt. I was so satisfied with my eternal present, I had long since forgotten what hope was. In a good way.

•

Then I started to become parched.

The coyotes yelped all night. After the fires, the trees were blackened to tree-shaped charcoal. The dust swirled around me on the morning hike. I might have been in the desert, except for the eleven million people spread below. Nor anyone at my shoulder to say, All this can be yours.

Of course, a burning bush would be just the ticket.

I couldn't go without sleep, so I had to find courage each night, in entering it.

Then I would glide through my days, whispering words like *buttercup . . . Jiminy Cricket . . . paralysis . . .* just to hear the sounds. I knew they had a magic energy, and that eventually, when I had said them enough, they would go away.

Lover and friend hast thou put far from me.

The season began to change: that meant, to drop into itself. The pool filled with pine needles. I spent time just skimming the surface.

Absinthe and tequila rolled like treacle down the ice luge. Inert substances, but on contact with the human I observed their flammability. My blood knew that all things are experienced, once if not many times, and that one can make room for, and rest calmly with, all that is to be experienced. But I felt like an observer, and I longed to be lost.

My blood knew everything. My head knew little. I longed to be lost: in battle.

Also every night: the distant freight trains rattled and blared. Yet another childhood dream fulfilled. I was ticking them off. Wasn't life grand?

I have gathered the myrrh and spices,
I have eaten from the honeycomb,
I have drunk the milk and the wine.
Standing outside the flow of things,

I noticed how lonely I'd become.

She said: *I want to talk to you, at roughly four removes.*

For a long time I walked away from dreaming. Gripping the wheel on the freeways.

Will I eat the flesh of bulls, or drink the blood of goats? Such irony in decision-making.

I admired, from my deckchair, the green hills of my peripheral turbulence.

I needed to choose to weep, or to watch football, so I chose football, because my instinct was to stay blank until further notice.

The cells bubbled silently in my liver. I was my actions not my thoughts, and longing is never love, and absence cannot be hate.

But the bones can ache.

•

Emerging into the interglacial from the glaciation of my distress.

I tried to climb into her but she gave no traction.

The blood became needy. I went to bed sick.

Night after night, the utter deprivation, because I was very good at sabotage.

If I had foregone the domestic energies, why then did they rise up to devour me?

Down the mountains over there, the car headlights flowed like lava.

The soupy schist from thirty thousand feet. I saw where the ice age had been. Hindsight, though: not exactly the same as wisdom.

•

All the girls started saying one thing and doing another. So I was learning ethics, backwards.

Everything that could sting, would sting.

The universe was animate, and showing its intent. I took everything personally.

The plains were endless, the planet vast. But even sorrow came around in a circle.

Harmania. The country where I lived. Ambiguous patriot. I will tether my rowboat here: Harmania.

I often cried at night in dreams, those private myths of plaintive distress. On the other hand, O Consolation of Israel, I was happy to be a multidimensional participant.

May I bless also the utter desolation which fell upon me. And even my ruination was one of God's names.

The mind in freefall, so full of *stuff.*

I was greatly anointed, with willow and aniseed. I went for long walks, the marjoram, the myrtle, the coriander garlands. I was back where we began this, the dogs half-wild, half-wold at my feet, preparations for winter including, but not limited to, the construction of a cabin, Eros come melt in my mouth, Eros sit heavy on my shoulders.

But that girl who worshipped the sun, without melancholy, without irony, she was lighter than a celery stick.

•

(Anakreon) And then to be so gracious with,
O loving friend, your slender thighs.

5

Walking the perimeter of the bogland, I saw how fat the earth was with its dead. O death-fat earth, give me that hard dry crust a moment more.

Down by the shoreline, I saw how oiled the sea was with its drowned. O sucking sea, hold off on that king tide another tide.

Out in the desert, I saw the way the dust invaded socks. (I felt the chafing of the underworld.) O desert sands, be damp with dew. O let me live.

I didn't burn to rule.

The injections had put me in shock. But I was eager to love.

•

My Loulou your heart was my barracks.

Thus said the great Apollinaire

Soaking wet by Hadrian's wall
I dreamed of sunlight and olive trees
And a comfortable pair of sandals.

Thus said the wise old Wystan Hugh

I was the recurring monad, featureless, passing through all those bodies, lilting through the centuries.

I saw the girls, as Archilochos saw,
Just budding into supple line.

Your fine, hard, bared crotch, he said.

(When I was an old goat patrolling the boundary fence I remembered I'd had dark, thick hair, a lustrous coat, and I hadn't known what it meant. Then all the injections thinned my blood, and with it my hair, and thus my Great Goat Self. An awkward self-goodbye and self-forgetting. Clattering over the rocks.)

And time sped up. O Gasoline of God, O Lord of Hosts, you greatly sped up time as it followed that one direction. You invented that word *relentlessly*, deliberately.

•

I had a post-exilic slump, returned covered in glory, my heels bled raw on the pricks of the palms, and the little detail of riding into town on my donkey was anti-climactic but what did I care I was moving into my centre. What is it that supports you in the face of total disaster? No other animal knows of itself between the cosmos and death. I was drunk with sex. I floated to the diner on the corner.

Time passes in
new countries

I was aware that the words still existed; just not in me. A phenomenon known as 'embracing the immanent'. The totem pole knows many things, the totem one great thing.

•

Belly to belly I rammed you, your little whimper like a sounding sea.

Strangeness of girlfriends in Harmania

She said she wanted to be like an interior designer—but inside people's souls. She had the radiance of California to back her up.

Her stupidity was all her own, though.

'Like' an interior designer—O Infinite One, O Restorer, O Guide, O Enricher, you let people like that give metaphor a bad name.

She was blossoming into her sillihood. She became the queen of that land.

But where was I?

Her doe-wide eyes were mild.

I came on her like a ton of bricks. You what?

•

Your fine, hard, bared crotch.

I would hold your hand, but the ship went down despite.

•

Lobony csbians of the hinternet. Okay then. Snap out of it. *Inter ubera mea commorabitur.* A bundle of myrrh is my beloved to me. He shall lie between my breasts.

Her doe-wide eyes were mild. No challenge there.

Lightning out behind the San Gabriel mountains. Ninety-nine stations on cable. A dog barking until dawn. On a bad night, re-runs of *Cops* were the pinnacle of all my capacities.

My peripheral vision began to spin.
Was this to say
That life was opening out, or closing in?

An I has weight, and sinks.

(Donne)   *All day the same our postures were*
And we said nothing, all the day.

(She was caught unawares by guilt; it didn't fit her
saintly self-image of selfless forbearance.)

(School of Basho)   *Picking mushrooms on*
The misty mountaintop,
No one knows where I am.

(I was caught unawares by rupture, though I had it
coming, in the sense that everyone does.)

(Saint-Exupéry)   *It is always in the midst, in the epicentre of your*
troubles that you find serenity.

(A voice rang out, a small clear voice. I knew nothing.
I gave up everything.)

I decided these would be the last words I would write on the subject. Even though I didn't write them.

I realised her world was so small. What a sad liberation! Then mine had been too.

But how can we sing the world song

In a strange land?

•

There were at least eighteen adjectives that could qualify
the word lottery, none of them 'groin'.

II

6

A voice rang out, a small clear voice. All over the planet the olive trees shook. The mountains and the buildings dripped with age. The little tales distorted through the years. The centuries piled up. Millenia. The battles ran with blood. I knew nothing. I gave up everything.

I answered thee in the secret place of thunder.

I cried for mercy for my body. My life was a vapour.

Running, but not away. The muscles burned. I thought I would explode.

I didn't know which way to turn. Metabolism was a fortress. Incoming, incoming.

For a very long time I could not breathe, and all I could hear was the drumming in my head. There were torrents inside me, they all caused pain. God put all the bad drivers on the streets at the same time.

Seer of All Knowledge, you put all the bad drivers on the streets at the same time. The car was a weapon. Its menace filled the world with wonder. Small mercies, and pedal to the medal.

There was no escape, but of course I tried to find it. Then I could not stop. Then I lost my freedom. Day by day the hours evaporated; hour by hour my hair fell out. Then everyone and everything was gone, except for whatever was most inappropriate. I could not be trusted to drive; there were no bad drivers, only me. Rage peppered the weeks.

•

I gave up the ghost. I was austere, in all my dealings with the world. There was nothing but the frenzied buzzing of the swarms of molecules. My hearing was perfect. It was perfectly annoying:

God put all the chewers in the restaurants beside me at the same time. I could hear you all swallow. I could hear the false teeth clacking. In my horror. I could not be trusted to eat.

I was flat and austere, there was nothing inside me. There were days it was so very pleasant.

•

But I am getting ahead of myself. First, bewilderment. So we praised the automobile or anger, whichever came first on any given day: even before ignition, Lord, I prayed to you, Let someone cut me off; just give me an excuse. For there is no limit on heaven or on earth to what the interference may concoct.

Will I drink the blood of goats?

•

The devil showed me cities of gold but I said No, I have
pedestrians to smash.

•

My life became small when my breath became short.
Event piled on event till all event
Conspired to prove how very small
The smallness could become. A thin
Clear voice in the desert said: Absurd.

A thin clear voice in the desert said, of emptiness: *This emptiness is huge.*

•

Being in the water would help. Such nakedness.

My head hurt on the inside. My scalp simply fled crust by
crust on the wind. I remembered when I was young and
beautiful. Before time turned elastic.

I am forgotten as a dead man out of mind. I am like a broken vessel.

7

Her form, okay, a violin. Lift up our hearts. From troubled dreams, the smell of acetate.

Red of the orange juice, blood of secretions, algal wasteland of the liver. Everything blood red today.

Liver and river: ridiculously interchangeable words. Like spaded clods of earth, all mulchy with moistness of dying.

The clock is counting down to the day. Everything red but for those pink pills.

A needle tunnels into the thigh. This is what you'll do now. But alternate the thighs, to avoid rash. Nurse says I'll teach you how to use a syringe. You say that sounds good. She says jack back to make sure there's no spume of blood. You say *No* spume of blood. Eyebrows arched.

•

Deep in the water of my first understanding
Blackness came upon me.
It stayed through all the long September days.

•

So keenly one exits this life where the living cluster. Their stalks are as silk; sunwards they are bending. God yearns for their yearning.

There is the pleasant emptiness of the large mind, unused.

There is the cracking of knuckles. There is unease. There is alarm not quite felt.

Thrombosis. Salutation. Every shrivelled gland had tried to pulse. Every seed had pushed through darkness. Every sticky sequence, every curving thought had curdled.

Thumble runders.

A doctor delves his hand into your neck. Pulling out all those needles. Up to his arms in it. Each week he finds that vein again: to take the traffic outwards. How life surprises, such changes of direction, if you stick around. Memories of milk and honey, O Most High.

If nausea is an ocean the bed is a ship, adrift on it.

Saliva rankling like acid.

The blood is gone from me today.

•

The murmurous riffles of the heart which is a muscle. The clear and pleasant pulsing of the brain which is a pressure. A southerly front brings rain, all night, at last.

It is 'snug', this life, but a little hard to breathe.

Of bounty, or the rains of fortune: every day a little less descends. But the sweetness of a waiter will undo you: lighting a candle at dusk when you can read no more. And yet every day, somewhere, that same dusk passes through Death Row.

It is a flooded world, but sick with shallow corpuscle.

•

A door bangs in the wind. All night. All night, a door bangs in the wind. Nobody does anything about anything and a plague has been sent upon me. There are other ways of making a decision but this one that tightens the chest, crawls the skin, wakes the deep sleep into slivers of racing thought or the solace of the imbecility of the infomercial, the blue hum of night, the disoriented hum of the sleeping masses, and drags you into day where even light hurts—well, why not? It is one of many. It is the one for now. Almost everything has a reason.

The year, rolling by, in its cellular decay, testing the guy-ropes of isolation, the transom guys and the bulwark guys and even the whisker guy. The brain lives on water. You are dumb as an ox or a kite. She is planning to leave.

Plasma the condition of a world without volition. Consciousness resides in oxygen. These are the starving times.

I borrowed from the library a book, a kind of amulet, to protect me from bloodshed on my journey. But there was bloodshed every day.

8

The luminous meets the tenuous; Lord, hear our prayer.

•

Not love or sleep. Certainly not sleep.

My uselessness blazed out its glory.

By now I had become most expert at internalising all my venom. I saved the best hatred for myself. In restrooms all over the world I spat and snarled. In transit lounges everywhere I knew my death was upon me soon.

•

But as for me, my feet were almost gone, my steps had well nigh slipped.

It was just another day of forward movement.

My blood took its long service leave.

The cabin crew stowed my medicine in a fridge.

Those of my friends who didn't believe
In violence believed in power.

That man was no longer an artist
But a bald angry motherfucker.

I thought perhaps everyone had joined the CIA.

*Rebuke the
company of
spearmen, the
multitude of the
bulls: scatter
thou the people
that delight
in war.*

9

It was sad, but at least consistent, that I would always be approximately five hundred million seconds older than her.

For a while I stopped being filled with wonder. This was merely disrespectful rather than Satanic. I had consonants, but could not get loose with the vowels.

I had the vapours. I looked inwards. I didn't read the physics of the matter. I stopped short of awe because now I didn't have the breath for awe. I had a debt of gratitude but I stopped short of being stabbed by the now. Nothing was *here*. It was all just panting.

To make matters worse I hustled everyone to exhaustion.

It was embarrassing to be so badly thought of. It was a big day. It was a small day.

Rooster long gone.

It was all just lumps of bodies in the dark.

She was dead in the eyes.

My blood went cold then went away.

I said my prayers for my brother.

I hoped that the beautiful women of Prague and Marseilles
would lead me to peace.

10

But I am getting ahead of myself. First, bewilderment. I had had a bad history with excess of happiness, and there had been a darkness. My mind never functioned the same way again. I thought as a child and I wrote as a child and for children. Effectively. God having said Eat whatever the Hell you want: but not from *that* tree.

Well, then: bewilderment, protein-enriched. To the filigree glory of God. In the very first seconds the atoms began to decay.

•

The Museum of Medieval Torture. I went with the flow of the flummox. It was no way to be a tourist. I was a disgrace even to the lonely.

I wrote not to create but only to respond. Because I was a changed man: lesser than before. I prayed for it to be a phase. But the whole world found itself in 'reduced circumstances'.

I flew into London, God help us all.

I liked structure and rhythm, I had fear in my life, I needed guidance, but clearly not to the point of Scientology.

11

So wonder now competes with microbial anxiety. But I've only so much space to go around. Preburstile behind every membrane, blood teeters and wobbles, constantly on the brink of its flowing or drying up. But now, O Grand Improvisor: since I'm not in my breath or my blood I am nothing for now and the mind (I am not in my mind) says *this is for always.* Says *there is nothing that is you.*

Once, I had welcomed the news.

So I flew through clouds, with my blood on the brink. That day, those nineteen men had more belief than me that day, which only goes to show, Eli Eli, how suspect belief is. Killing all those people without their permission.

Possibly jetlagged, I stood in the hardware store, gazing at all the gleaming *tools of surrender.* The *quoi*?

•

I lost my balance in the world;
I had so much desire to turn so wrong.

I was a ghost in this place called World.
So much desire to turn, and be, so wrong.

I had no body no nothing.
No likelihood.

I yearned for a base in this place called World. The belly
the belly the belly the belly the belly the belly the base of
the world.

12

So weary we tread this land where the mountains tumble.
Wearily we trod. How gladly we enter this life where the
living crumble.

Why would we like birdsong but not the rumbling and
groaning of the caterpillar? Because everything works
to scale.

I was trying—breathlessly, O Provider of Mountains—
To understand the difference between symbol and image,
Allegory and thought-form, since life dispensed coherence,
A hilarity of madness, a wind through history calming,
On sunny fields of mud-dried metaphor:
I was baffled by the Bacaudae,
Bemused by the Burgundians, the Alamans
Confounded me, the Goths and Visigoths
Within, the Britons and Thuringians:
All fought fiercely inside of me:
I was all of Gaul, beset, a knot of conflicts.
The Suevic kingdom held the Frankish to ransom.
Five brands of Vandals for every Lombard.

The Austro-Hungarian fucked with the Taliban.
All that mayhem in the mud.

By day above the battlefield:
The violence of the butterflies.

At night I imagined a maiden's breasts,
Or many, many maidens.

By day such abandon to the sword.
Gorge rose with battlestench.

O the bounce, O Lord,
Of those dreams in the battle-tent.

•

I cried out then to Yahweh:
Great Answerer,
When I die will I die
Related to anyone?

A cloud spoke:
Before all death
You need to learn
If you *can* be related to anyone.

•

Was he talking about permission or ability? It took oxygen
to answer questions like that. I dragged myself heaving
through the more basic tasks.

47

13

When I remember these things, I pour out my soul in me.

In everything there is there's sound not silence. The atoms roar, wheeling and frictionless. The atoms plummet through the tympanic membrane, and a while later through the cupula. There is no resistance. There is nothing fine enough. There is nothing that registers. But everything is roaring.

Everywhere I went I built structures of reverence.

The neutrinos pass straight through the atoms. I am no longer made up of me.

If the neutrino, in its endless vibrating, as it pierces all spaces, could ever find molecules of air on which to make its humming felt, on which to simply register, then all would be so deafening we'd be distracted in the end. What I took to be silence, my Illustrious Father, was at most just distance from my ears, and you plucked me, as a harp, to sleep, when we slept by the haystacks when the harvest was done, when I ate metaphor like light but was starved for a good carrot. Illustrious Father, now hear my prayers.

•

When she leaves, you do not fret, for she too will learn
she was born just to prove that loss is final, that to live
is to die. We all rejoice, or not. Rejoicing is hardly the
point. Travailing in birth, and pained to be delivered, we
released ourselves in solace. In the stress of the years
which followed, we forgot. Lord, slap us round again. Be
kind to her; she is equally to be loved. I cannot breathe;
I cannot be the lover.

14

Her form, okay, lift up your heart.

From troubled dreams, the smell of acetate.

Deep familiarity with the geography of the hospital. By the third month, once the bones were up to their elbows in it, then I became bone-weary.

There is not in this world anywhere a helpline, not even a hospital helpline, will assuage the sourness, the psoriasis of time; we simply peel away.

I cried to the world I am yours and my dreams are yours, but I had no idea, not a clue, what surrender was, prostrate on the floor of my narcissism. I was still an imbecile. The extravagant freedom of second-by-second capitulation eluded me.

I always snapped back up. Upright and hard alee. Lord, snap me back down again.

•

From troubled dreams, the smell of acetate. The membrane through which inner and outer exchanged their currency was now known as the syringe. Medicinal use only. I had long since forgotten its ways. And now you are a 'good boy', like a dog.

All these disguises of zero. The Self unadorned.

It was in my bones. There were only moments.

All my desire is before thee; and my groaning is not hid from thee.

Pinnately arranged on a central stalk was a version of wild and haunting beauty. I was so long off the game it took some time for the word to take shape on my lips: *flower.*

My heels bled raw on the spongy ground. Joy surprise sorrow anger fear disgust: these were said to be the emotions.

•

We went through fire and water, O Merciful One, yet you have brought us forth to a spacious place.

15

That there was a structure, even to the blood, was thinness of consolation as it thinned to broth. One sipped anaemically at life.

For the thing which I greatly feared is come upon me.

For the arrows of the Almighty are within me, the poison whereof drinketh up my spirit.

All the while my breath is in me, and in my nostrils life arrives. And leaves.

My bones are pierced in me in the night season: and my sinews take no rest.

Thou dissolvest my substance.

But through the pitch and drag of days, O Thou Who Art Present, I chanced upon the sporadically excellent. I was made humble to hear that the horse had clothed his neck with thunder. He pawed in the valley and mocked at fear and did not turn away from the sword. He swallowed the ground with his rage. He smelled the thunder of the captains, and the shouting.

God, how I needed good role models.

Then the desert was filled with hummingbirds.

Then I was filled with desert.

The desert came with instructions. Spread your arms wide to the mountain lion. Walking backwards but not looking backwards. Huh? I really needed to minimise the instructions. All the while alert for rattlesnakes. Existence was complex. Moreso without much oxygen.

My life, like a bird, has escaped
The snares of the fowler.

I have no love for the halfhearted,
My love is for the whole.

Let us pray. *I missed a girl I could not help but miss.*
Such missing was colossal in the face
Of all the tender hours that came to pass,
Yet I was stranded there as if in space,
And had no gravity, because no mass.
I missed the girl I could not help but miss,
And all the tender hours that came to pass
Seemed hollowed out and lessened by the loss.
Forgot the rules I learned when I was young.
I missed a girl I could not help but miss.

I miss what I have not permission to miss.

The floods have lifted up their voice; the floods lift up their waves.

Farewell to one future, and welcome the water.
Welcome the heft of rejoice.
Take what is found in front.
Work with available blood.

III

16

When I woke in the snows I knew, though I would die, that it would not be yet. I resigned myself to, and looked forward to, the dissolution of the molecules, a specific act of which I had vividly dreamed. I was overjoyed that I would fight a battle still. That I would narrow down the tasks: one thing, then one. That I would take in my immediate surroundings: the way beauty funnelled here— *wherever one was!*—and clung to itself, and replicated, and gathered momentum. Even while it, and we, were on our way to death.

We'd make a merry jaunt of it.

I was closing the gap between life as I lived it and one that was waiting. Even flight. What expansion.

All this was called the grace of the Heir of All Things.

Yet at times all I could do was look forward to coming out the other side of the inner fearin'; what else but knuckle down?

In the kingdom of the blood tests

As for the emotional essentials: O the stark luxuries, O Prime Mover.

The scores of galaxies all around, and the large expanses of time. Why all the fuss, and pain? I really had to rein in that self-obsession. Note to self.

And yet first the white blood cells, then the red, took leave of absence. In the end even thoughts are a luxury. There was what, *plasma* flowing through me?

Just another day of forward movement. My uselessness blazed out its glory.

Such grand sadness inside her, I mean me.

I was moving very slowly through my tasks. One thing, then one.

A doctor said: you can do your treatment, or your life, but not both. I told him I would be the exception to the rule. He said you are not listening. He said you will lose one thing, at least, like sanity, or love, or health. He was right. Her holiday became emigration, and then I knew I was a third-world country like any other. Developing industries I'd forgotten I'd needed to develop.

I had to emerge from all those injections that refused to prolong my life. So then I had to make time go slower, by living it faster. Relativity.

So many aeroplanes, breathing their peace into me, but still I could never qualify for those frequent flyer miles. No one would upgrade me, and I was forever projecting

my anxiety forwards to the fat man in the middle seat.
On the next flight.

Impinging on my airspace, which was often all that I had.

•

I began to pray, for all of us, each morning. *O Witness,
O Word: how gladly we enter this life where the living
crumble.*

I began to understand time as a catchment area. Myself
in it. The endless rain, and the possibility one might be
soaked and functional all at once.

I'd make it to the coast, and understand time differently
at last.

*The earth and all
the inhabitants
thereof are
dissolved.*

I had not fallen into waters where I could not swim; I swam
in those waters with ease. This made me, apparently,
a mystic, though I broke out in rashes at the injection
sites, and I could never remember if yesterday was left
stomach or right thigh.

I would not pretend to be better than others, since that
was the very worst kind of pretending. I would offer my not
pretending to God, Image of God, the Sanctifier, He Who
Is Present, the Man of Sorrows, the Strong One Who Sees,
Who Coverest Himself With Light as With a Garment—

—God, thou gift of God.

I wanted to get to the place called *Slightly Tilted*; the Vedas
had told me it exists.

•

All day, with the rain, I was good with that.

The persistence
of memory

Though the skin rankled, the rain made good its promises,
so constantly extravagant, and I was always soaked, at
least in spirit, and you were always wet, it goes without
saying, in that ideal world, which is gone.

•

The rest was blood. One thing eating another in the blood.
The silence of the self as the self eats itself.

Doctors and
nurses are
generally
enthusiastic in
their progress
reports

You inject a foreign superbody. A chemical superhero. How
grand is its work. It wipes out cities in its wake. Didn't
know its own strength. Making me scorched earth.

Denuding me of sense, and love, of entire invisible cities
in this little strip of time. But as reincarnating monad,
I went through bodies; put them on and took them off, as
clothes. I was transparent and neutral: but I came into
existence with my faults, and gladly so, a seething mass
of neutrons trapped in the substance of the world. For
which, read void.

A ring around the moon. A plane flew through the ring.
Anoint me with every oil, O Thou Who Hast Gathered
the Wind in Thy Fists. The earth is the tabernacle of its
own transcendence. When I worked that out, it offset the
sadness of speed.

•

I was living at the boundaries of myself. How both to live and remember immediacy.

The paradox of hospitals

I went on a world tour of kindness. From Big Sur you could see Sydney, if not for the small issue of horizons, which are the infinite expression of the earth's curvature, and thus create missing, as well as forward intention. No one knew me on my world tour, so I could be gentle everywhere, and still experience personal greatness.

Over tea and toast and a boiled egg in another foreign city, reading the morning paper, I was not so far from Tintin after all. It was pretty much what childhood thought it would be, though in practice the three-dimensional details, the component parts of actuality, tend to fill themselves out as they go. O Horn of Salvation, dispensing abundance.

The consensus is you can call that life.

Yet certain parts of life mattered far more than others. I had never been overly concerned with money, which was only at best an energy to be shifted. I was kind even to myself.

Every city was a fortified city. Such steadfast love. Every village was a fort. I felt protected every time I came in from the desert.

Thou crownest the year with thy bounty; thy paths drip fatness.

All thy garments smell of myrrh, and aloes, and cassia, out of the ivory palaces, whereby they have made thee glad.

17

When my swollen tongue burst into speech I was slurring my words but I found gist and rightness.

Lamb of God, you take away the peccadilloes of the world.

I climbed up and above myself, like a tree. Then I climbed above the tree.

I was 'gifted', in one way only, but in many more ways than one.

The world went on, with all its trials. God came smashing through the middle:

Forgiving us our peccadilloes.

18

No one could accuse me of taking the symbol for the
substance; but you could drown in symbol;

So I tried to climb into the world; but it gave no traction.
Then I drove up into the mountains. Above the snow line, Sangre de Cristo
my friends knew death deeply. Their daughter had ejected, Mountains
to a world of sound, from her world of silence, but there
was only one great sound, then she was gone. Their lost
love had somewhere to go: through time. They knew it
deeply.

•

Nor was I in any way or at any time inoculated from the
experience of the real, though if wishes were dreams,
I would own an orchard. Thus, O Alpha, O End, small
mercies abounded. Though it was a long time since I'd sat
under the shade of a coolabah tree, watching in mirage
the stockman watching endless time, even as he knew,
dreaming only of life, that his own was not endless.

LUKE DAVIES

*They gave me
also gall for my
meat; and in my
thirst they gave
me vinegar to
drink.*

Let it dissolve, the endless gravity. Time disappeared. The doctors said only seven months to go.

19

I wandered down to the marsh. Even the frogs had quietened for winter. Snow clouds in the starting stalls, neighing with energy, snorting their imminence, ready to burst.

The world in all its electrical discharge, its permanent state of crackle. Conquering Lion, you gave us the gift of the passage of time; your proper due was gratitude;

Yet for however long gratitude's frequency was low (it was lower even than the background radiation, and lower than background hum), we would have to put up with war.

I knew the blizzard was coming. In the meantime you could hear a pine needle drop. The sedge had all but withered from the lake. One good thing out of three would have to do. I had promises to keep.

Daily I was daring more or all.
One good thing out of three would have to do.

•

But no one ever talked, when talking about the pantheons, of the comedic deities: Vedic, Greek, Norse, Hebrew or otherwise. God's prayer was always *May it be my will that my mercy be greater than my anger.* Nothing about *my sense of humour.*

•

Zero degrees
Kelvin, even pain
is waylaid by
the languid
absurdity of
existence itself

And a small voice cried out,
But it was loud, because I had invited
So much space into my life,
Until every dew-drop's *pop* was crisp,
And the atoms so languidly roared,
And the hopper-grass made the *hop,*
And the humming-bee made the *hum,*
A small voice cried out:

I am black time, come to lick up all man,
And you must be unafraid.
I am black time, come to lick up all man,
And you must be unafraid,
With all your heart, of chit, and chat.
I am black time, come to lick up all man,
And you must be unafraid,
With all your heart, of what, and where, you are.
You must fight your battle.

Out, distraction.

20

Luke's mind got cleansed by the Salinas River
Now everyone follows, saying *Luke, Luke*

This was how religion began.

•

O Father of Mercies,
Heir of All Things,

Horn of Salvation,
There is no greater love than your laughter:

Your will was not the world
But the world is thick with will.

•

I knew about the spin in electrons
I knew about uncertainty at the subatomic level
So I should have known better about loss.

But brains were so oxygen-poor that the world
Self-congealed in perplexity's salts
And the conflict between inside and outside raged on.

When the fog rolled in, the mountains disappeared.
They too had been an illusion of certainty.
I decided to forego womanhood. Or rather, women.

•

Briefly, he
imagines a
different future

It wasn't deep time, but it felt like a long time to us: moss on the cottage roof. The dream of the enduring garden.

Once we could relax, after all those billions of years of jostling stresses, we were able to feel that a few hundred years was substantial, and that families meant longevity.

I lay under a giant oak tree. The summer was kind.

•

I sat on a plinth for a very long time: nine months at least, or years perhaps. Not well, but dealing with it. I came out of myself. I left myself, or left myself behind. O God of Sorrows, O Buddha of Snows, in the trade journals this is known as happy destiny.

Lord, Lord, avoid for me then the screeching of metal. Or rather, do my avoiding. Protect me.

21

So anyway, O Word, O Witness, O Diadem of Mercy:

Then I got a *grrr* happening.

It had become the bloodhead, rather than the godhead.
Or I, rather.

Memory and strategy were moving towards something
very much like intelligence. I waited long ago, by the
waterhole, for the violent event.

But I waited in peace, so I meditated too.

This was before television burst the levees of discourse.

Cable in particular did me over. I confused sunrise with
moonrise.

But I shook some sense into myself, and deep underground,
where I burrowed so long, I found nutrients in the tubers,
and something in me stirred.

22

I took a journey from Jerusalem to Babylon. The great city was not as bad as I had been led to believe, and there was a mall on every block. I felt just as at home as when I had travelled through Urbud and Ute. In Babylon I told myself I bathed in some Euphrates of the mind; small birds twittered and splashed in the birdbath outside the window.

Simple prayer for a new country

O Liberator, I make my day a prayer to you. May I be soft within it, by your grace.

Such clarity of loss, even in the angles,
Especially in the angles, such brittleness of light.

O I've found no answers and they'd be no help at all.

Daylight was a desert, the world a sandstorm. Low visibility kept me guessing at the forms of things.

May all be well. May the true me be revealed to the Babylonians. Safe landings, happy travels.

23

I'd skipped a generation on myself, autumn evening foot-
ball pick-up, the baseball diamond and the raked leaves.
How easily only one path becomes possible. Such is life.
I missed, but not without relief, those curves of wealth in
tree-lined streets, the peace of driving home enclosed, and
no loose tapping in the cylinders. I skipped that generation
when I blinked. There I'll come when I'm a man, with a
camel caravan.

I see those portly men with portly wives. The history of
tennis lessons. The sacrifices. They are younger than me.
It is inconceivable. Life. I have eyes for their daughters.

I had seen the world from upside-down. I had admired
Jughead's bedroom. I had lived lifetimes in atlases. I had
frequented dusty diners. Take me out to the ball game.
I had imagined many futures but never interferon. I had
watched so many movies under the protection of 3 a.m.
and the benediction of dawn. I had dreamed of such
vastness that somehow I floated, adrift between planets,
for years. I was king of the stateless. I came down from

*He breaketh the
bow, and cutteth
the spear in
sunder; he
burneth the
chariot in
the fire.*

the mountain. The unattainable girls became attainable women. O Keeper of Scales, balance Thou mine heroics. I had horses to ride. I was mad acanter on the floodplain of my fortunes. My pain was compulsory, but with the right saddle, the suffering was optional. Then I hocked my saddle, because when I was young, I was often foolish.

24

When the peace left the high I found myself
At last betrayed and self-estranged.
But by what? I simply woke up every day;
I had at some point given my life to narcosis.
I was utterly faithful and yet
It had told me every day that I was nothing.
I tried to trace prayer back which after all
Was shaky thankyous in the night-nothings too
While sabre-tooths paced puzzled
By the fire from the blackness,
But everything became confused, the rivers running
With blood, the curse of the Canaanites,
Did Lilith come before Eve and so forth:
God take it, I said, the self-agony too.
Everything worked as antivenene.
O Lord who is Present,
I was worthless day after day
(Or rather: I was nothing,
Filling myself with all those holes,
Beating the night with sticks).

The deep
evolution of
memory

Small demons had long
Hung around me in clusters
Saying *this man will feed us; O this man*
Will certainly feed us. It took a long time
But at last they became hungry and bored.
Sighing, they dispersed. Furthermore a man
Wrapped himself up in a very small package;
I had some serious string to untie.
Holy Toledo.

•

God hath made
me to laugh,
so that all who
hear will laugh
with me.

God has made laughter for me and all—

•

I sat straight-backed so as to reconnect
With my own handwriting.

At a certain point a certain lightness left
My shoulder blades.

That's not quite right.
It was the weight that went.

•

A very long time earlier (seven thousand generations)
juniper had indeed been the wick of the cave.

The Passage of
Time

Then, by the time we began praising the Lord from the
earth, ye dragons, and all deeps, fire and hail, snow and

vapours, stormy wind fulfilling His word, mountains and fruitful trees and all cedars, it was high civilisation indeed. Then suddenly there were motorcars too.

So little blood. So little oxygen. I couldn't stand myself or my life. But I reduced that to more sensible levels, so that in the end I couldn't stand things like evil. And after a while, stupid people. Or theft. Tasteless fruit. Anything with cinnamon in it.

Eleven months and counting

Manageable disdain, O Father of Mercies.

•

On the other hand I loved bodies of water, the deeper the better.

I had the strength of a bear that had the strength of two bears.

If truth be told

In Eridanus: the imprint of another universe on our own. A long river rolling from the foot of Orion, sweeping south of Taurus, in the Heavenly Waters, to the far edge of Cetus. Phaeton stole a chariot from Helios, he of the sun, but was not used to such torque; he donutted out of control, lost the vehicle to the waters. His shame in the reeds. A cold patch in the water or a large galactic void. The languid hippo did not blink an eye.

The bells, keeping time. I offered them to you, or you to me it was all the same, the bells the final sound in space. I closed my eyes. The molecules dispersed. I felt myself spreading. I was always coherently me, just a little more

He had experienced death before, and dreamed of it yet to come.

diluted in the end. That was how the universal soul came into being, because the elasticity of goodness was limitless. The molecules dispersed. Each part of me kept saying goodbye to the other, without loss.

The single-heralded comet came. Significance everywhere, but nothing like schizophrenia. I found myself in single-handed combat. The symbols fought well, but never overpowered me. I woke each dawn victorious.

The world received us into its citizenship. I trod the road to Jericho. We lay down. We wept. The buildings all fell down. And even my blood, O Thou my Redeemer, was yearning for water, as usual.

Parched. The desert parched. The parched lips on the flower buds. The cactus yielded syrup of the mind.

I imagined lying between her legs.

Certain thoughts were sustaining. It had always been like that.

Her fine, hard, bared crotch.

Plus, on your death bed you would not remember any particular tax return over another.

It wasn't as if I had to sing like thunder; it's just that inside my throat, there really was a rumbling down the ages, and a vibration in which I experienced, rather than understood, peace. The end of all *our* and all *that*. I vibrated into a ball of light.

Because I had chosen to turn my attentions in a certain direction. There was no greater mystery, Lord, except that all was mystery. Rejoicing was hardly the point, since it was the only point.

Respite in adversity

I felt my days flow on.

I was mute in situations when it mattered, and so I learned loneliness, a year or two. That wasn't so much fate of my own devising, more that you can't always be lucky. Can't always be at ease. And yet *Blessed are we who feed at the table of grace.*

Then a small clear voice called out:
Cease striving
And know that I am God.

The acoustics of grace

My yoke will be easy:
Uttering the memory of great goodness.

•

Always the coming back to night
When I wrote so completely untroubled
By the city's alpha waves,
That low hum of docility at four a.m.,
Infinite Melbourne, or Baffin Island,
I was nearly frozen, nearly dead,
But something came into my blood,
And roiled (may it stop now, Lord) for years.
May I die without a debt to stupidity.

Down and out in Hardware Lane

As a dream when one awaketh, so, O Lord,
When thou awakest, thou shalt despise those images;
Emerging from the honeycomb of your pity
You shall shout with joy, because you can,
For the evidences of your wreckages,
For your god-created improbabilities
And for the improbabilities of confluences.

25

I returned to the poem, the one true place,
Whose blood was the syntax,   A love affair
Whose body was the word.

Thus I felt fortunate to have had
Much experience with blood.

Part of the challenge of being heroic:
The object of my desperation would desert me.
But the desperation wouldn't.

•

Matter evolved as the narrative of light.
Matter was the evolution of the narrative of light
Through time and space in the history of Being.
Waving my cutlass, I scythed the air.
(God bless this notebook and all who sail in her.)

•

I knew there was pain
But pain was not aching

She drank too much
She was bored with drinking

What I loved was the waiting
And the *almost* the *I'm lonely*

The *I dare you to amuse me*
The *Shall I fly to meet you*

The surrender the *I'm coming*
And the scar on her forehead

•

Could I reach the end of my body what beyond?
What beyond my body, and the blood?

Could I find the field where I *was,* and would always be?

I could see out of my eyeballs, but never the other side of
them. I could only think that. Then she had to go home.

•

I knew I wasn't permanent. It wasn't that. But I became
so temporary, even unto myself, that in losing my blood,
and the life I had known, I also lost the space in which
to think carefully, to act with care, to walk quietly. A lot to
be said for those quiet, deliberate steps. Redeem my exile,
Man of Sorrows.

Remove Thou this pain. My lips are blue. Fill Thou these lungs. Remind me of living.

It had always seemed that everything would burn me; I felt unclean.

Restlessly I understood, before God who was like a river to me, that restlessly in cheap hotels, deep in the middle of night, the room apace with thoughts, I understood, so restlessly, with retrospect, the why of drugs: I remembered thee, Zion, and the cedars. And I was a robber then too.

One discomfort recalls another

I was a robber and lost my youth to robbery. I cleaned out from my life big chunks of sky. I cleaned out swathes of sky, self, presence, picnics, grace; and all was felt as robbery.

Something essential was taken. All was revealed to be rolling loss. Something was always missing.

Daylight robbery. Even in daylight. The large galactic void.

•

What beyond the body and the blood? Or the hotel room with the view of the sky? And the night such a barrel of laughs.

I would still be waiting for the birth of syntax had we lain ourselves down. You were complete. Even your blushing was a complotion. Resistance was both everything and futile. In the intervals between catwalks you read the *Tractatus*.

The other models thought you were pretentious but you'd merely jumped the rusty gate from beautiful to curious, and Heidegger was next. The trick of leaving behind the banana plantations and the hippy communes and the past was to be glacially smart and tropically soft. You came down from the hills to devour the world.

Still, surrender had to be offset with 'slowly', which for an entire night, universes of it, was your catchphrase, even as you enacted great tenderness, even as yearning beckoned you gently. Then you lay so still, like a light-sponge, like a world-sponge. I had saved many metaphors for just such a moment. Even your blushing was blood and its signs.

You made of clothes an artform too, how they built up and pared down. There were buttons and chains and each thing matched, this lace with that breath, as if all was meditation, the entire universe and we, in it, all nothing but a hum.

I was learning new words all the time. Ignition.

A humming.

(Archilocus alexandri) A hummingbird found his way into the poem, look!

It sucked from the stamen of unease
Until unease was dry, and useless.

(de Caussade) I have no longer anything
To look after or to do.

26

My feet floated off the edge of the world, the Orkneys of your own soft dream of a half-closed eye in a half-lit room and a breath half-breathed: all in all, completeness that.

So I treated myself to touch, because there were wars everywhere, and even white noise was trademarked by now. You knew how to walk.

You wrote to me from England. Picnics filled with sun and nothingness. The dogless path to the smugglers' church.

•

Then I had to travel too. Such trances in airports at the foot massage. But what a way to fill in time. I felt myself on a golden bough. Then I felt myself asleep on a golden bough.

Be still, and know that I am God.

Death swims on the water,
Summer will soon be here.

Things were not always good. But when they were.

•

Elaborate Artificer, Zen God of the Baroque, all is yours,
all is from you and all is for you.

Mine is to be content with you and not adopt any one line
of action other than that which I'm in, which entangles
and untangles, which is best known as the life of action.
When one thing ends, I know it works. In a new place I
always recalibrate. It happens again and again.

I flowed for years with sense of understanding
That the gods would render all of this experience
Ecstatic. I had to show up.

There was a marvelous simplicity to the complexity with
which I chose to dress the days. Themselves memorials
to gods.

If you want to have fun, said God, go home and buy
yourself a monkey. Otherwise act with great purport.

No landing had been a crash landing so far in my life:
aviation statistic. From the faded galleys of the longships,
or the great banquet halls where thought became possible,
and laughter: sustenance emerged, called love. Holy crap
how one had to fight for it.

Be generous and loyal. Practise charity. These were not the
most innate of qualities. But with kindness came gratitude.
At that point even aeroplanes took on the character of
co-operative marvel.

A doctor's letter for the cabin crew!

The times may have suited my size. (I was small and mean by now, my body lost in sense memory.)

On horseback I felt the same echo for centuries too.

Overcoming. Overcoming. I overcame nothing. Least of all, quite clearly, time.

When the pilot said we were crossing the Delaware he was 'referencing' 'history'. Or was that the Potomac? Each time I came to new lands they were vast. But pulling back to the power of ten, space expanded till the earth shrank: this humming jewel, this emptiness. I too had found nobility in surrender, but it was a fine line. To overcome uncertainty was to accept it. We lay ourselves down by the waters. Nations came and went. But not this love.

One cannot afford to get stuck, at any given artery.

Believe in nothing you have been told, even if I have said it, you said, O Destroyer. Unless it coincides with your common sense. This is my voice, the voice said, after the thunder. But I was busy painting bison on the walls. The glaciers left behind them such arrays of rubble. Everything slowly petrified, but in petrifying fear, you have to pierce it.

•

I will abide, I said, a voice in the wilderness. I could sense many animals. Not only did the kingfisher catch fire but the fish fought back at the flames.

Then the salmon of wisdom was upon me. Abide in the mind of the unknown.

Every day I unrolled my groundsheet, the meadows vibrated, and space grew around me until I was comfortably small. All this was a way of telling the truth.

One year is thirty million seconds. An extravagant amount of everything to go round.

Death as both definitive rigidity and definitive unravelling

Non dolor est maior quam cum violentia mortis unanimi solvit corda licata fide. Heartbreak fucks you up like nothing else except the violence of death. It was time to move again.

She bid me burst my fetters.
And I did.

27

The more you sing of your desires,
The closer you'll get to Atlantis.
Atlantis has melons with edible rinds.
The biomass converter will turn anything to ice cream.   Southern
We ran low on song fuel. So then we sang some more.   California
We were so tiny, and breathless, and happy,
Beneath the vaulted arches.
Singing tra-la. Everything in perspective.
Deep beneath the inversion layer, Atlantis,
So softly sprouting palms. The dry summer evenings.
The blue jays sipping from the swimming pool.
It is an honour and a pleasure to welcome you to Atlantis.
We long ago gave up our obsession with wealth;
But feel free to fill up your pockets with our treasure.
(O I wish I'd dropped in at my tailor,
To make these pockets larger.)
Art is what happens when you learn to dream of
The universe's oldest bubble, so delicate, so floaty.

It is not a lost city
If you settle your heart.

●

So it wiped out everything, all praise the interferon. But there'd be no place to end, except that times in life are endings and beginnings, and some must be chosen as one or the other. Or else it's madness. If everything were to become anecdote, those for whom anecdote was central thrust would be lucky, in that the thrust of the here and now would render anecdote impermeable to fad. That is how we lived mythically, even as time rushed us like wind. Something to being stripped bare.

●

When I woke, when the picture broke up into its elements, I saw such thickness of sheer being. O, the world in general. O, such world.

●

A man in a long-standing trance
Somehow lived by the seat of his pants;
But the piper of rhyme
Pierced the bubble of time
And all that was left was expanse.

●

The tickertape became the teletext;
Without reference to the internet
I vaulted to telesthesia.

•

Conquering Lion, Gasoline of God, you asked so much of
me: *And this is the offering which you shall take of them:*
gold, and silver, and brass, and blue, and purple, and
scarlet, and fine linen, and goats' hair, and rams' skins
dyed red, and badgers' skins, and acacia wood, oil for
the light, spices for anointing oil, and for sweet incense,
onyx stones, and stones to be set in the ephod, and in the
breastplate, and let them make me a sanctuary; that I may
dwell among them. And there, above the mercy seat, I'll
meet with thee. I didn't know where to begin.

It wasn't that it was the dead zone. It was livelier than
that. But the barn swallows had no idea that the berries
were radioactive, so they chirped all day long from tree to
tree, in the forest primeval, and I wanted to say fly away,
fast and far, but of course I couldn't interfere with nature;
that was *your* job.

Likewise I was learning to accept, and not just endure,
disappointment. The same goes for joy.

IV

28

Counting bone and clavicle
For shape and cadence
The metres were on fire
Bowed head pursed lips
You counted syllables with fingers
And then for shape and cadence
Counted my ribs, another path
To contact, as I lay breathing

Asleep you whispered skeletons
Of phrases, the cadence of their bones

Great lilt from which great fall
Made all of life begin

While all around, the metres were on fire:
Constant state, velocity
Of the world, and time careening

●

The treatment
fails; great love
goes missing.
When all is
stripped away,
the first
important
insight that
remains: poetry

The second
important
realisation:
memory

I'd been in love with my cro-magnon life
Because I knew the plants
That took me outside my body
I knew I would kill the oryx the next day
And I did not care if I would die:
I loved the grand adventure, death so close.
I painted the memories of my altered state
On cave walls everywhere

But it was over, it was done. *Hallelujah*. (I needed a word
that was the bewilderment version of hallelujah, but
extensive research suggested it didn't exist.) Even the
thought of writing a goodbye letter made my blood stir,
since I thought it appropriate to ignore her volitions. The
thought of writing! Of writing one of those letters you don't
send. The kind that Alaric the Visigoth had never heard of.
(For all his faults, he came down on the side of the active.)

What would I say in that letter? That my blood was seven
years older. That the world was painted thus? That she
had come through the birth canal of her own idiocy? I'd
had a forceps birth myself and been a pinhead ever since;
the extended labour argument was not my strong suit. You
know all this, Great Knower. That I had sought to reduce
confusion. That the effort to survive her careless violence
was immense. That knowledge, by itself, is isolation.
That the particular, well-embraced, is not knowledge but
knowing. That she had not only loved me but desired
me. (She had written, 'This is what I am wearing when
you pick me up at the airport.') That terror before the
abyss of the self was not the same as the transcendent
in freefall. (She had written, 'You pull the dress over my

head.') That time collapsed in singularities. That you,
Great Knower, had loved the truth in dark places. That
you grafted wisdom onto mystery. That I became the vine
of that. That the future was see-through. That life was the
gap between oblivion and memory, and that the myriad
claims of bustle were thus all the more absurd. That my
blood was seven years older now. That the earth and all
the inhabitants thereof are dissolved. That I must find
kindness, even in my goodbyes, for everyone was weary,
and surely she not least.

•

I was elevated with luck   The third
We went together everywhere luck and me   epiphany: time
Luck swapping why for okay
The vertiginous became the everyday
The everyday the engine of existence
Luck in the brickwork of the minutes
These monuments of the fleeting

To your touch I bowed down
At your touch I bowed down

•

I called artillery into a woodline   The fourth
Where I received sniper fire   thing: war

Later hell we reported bodies
Where there weren't none

LUKE DAVIES

Water buffalo
Shadows

Children already dead from yesterday

Keepin the brass happy is all

•

The fifth
important
understanding:
the lost world

Adored with fire and lustral water

I hung nine nights on the gallows tree

In the next age I was forgotten

They called my grove Brocken

•

The sixth
important
moment: the
terms of death

Earth and hill all sweating now
Soon they'll become completely well

Badger came and crow and mouse
All kingdom of me in the forest
All kinds of men!
The tiger came to kill me
Because I am old

•

The seventh
great elation:
letting go

More than fog and more
Than all the flowers,
Love settled on the city like dew.

We thought we might walk
Into water or winter so melted
With heat was the dark heart of matter.

I'd long forgotten home but luckily
At moments when a glowing pierced the street
I landed, like a bird, inside myself.

One summer all the stones dissolved.
The planet too. The dandelions tumbled
Through the air. I yearned for dusk.

For a moment I imagined thunder
Crackling in the canyons.
Light billowed. The oceans heaved.

For every decade I toiled
A bird flew away from my hand
Into an empty sky.

There came a day I wept,
For the scent of jasmine,
For the taste of mango, for memory.

For every decade I toiled
There trailed me, like a brother,
A little lost, my glory.

A hot wind hinted of orchards.
The world grew weary with waiting.
Love settled on the city like loss.

For a long time I was dreaming
Of a stream trilling over rocks:
Dappled cool, dangling heels.

29

Elaboration of
the lost world

I know that I hung, on a wind-battered tree, for nine long
nights, and the day barely day, and the gloom of brooding
thunder, and the spear-wound weeping.

The Odin tree: so I offered myself to myself. I hung for nine
days, the tree howling.

No one knows where its roots begin. No one gave me food.
Not a horn of drink. When I looked down, the ground was
strewn with books, but the words were jumbled like runes.

I was up on the tree.

Down there, the roots of the runes.

I was as a burnt string: it looks like a string, but when you
blow, there is nothing there.

Nothing but tree. Nothing but wind.

Then I began to bear fruit. Then I began to know many
things. Then I began to thrive.

Word by word, I sought out words. Fact by fact, I sought out facts.

What to do when the treatment ends

I know songs which the king's wife does not know, nor the son of man, to guard you from your strifes and cares. Or rather, me from mine.

I saw strange visions, but this was only natural to one living so near the borders of the world.

•

I took to barren rocks, and preached to the fishes and the seabirds there.

My life was inconceivable even to me: its continuance, its reprieve. Better to live something rather than think it, I learned.

The seagulls made frenzy by the cliffs. The notion that one needed a certain IQ to experience one's loneliness with God was the fashion of the day. The bitter irony of the eremites. Being in your head does *not* mean being in your being.

30

So from all these physical events we wove (but weaving is so lame) a world of death.

The 'how' is opened;
Burn fold and fen.

I had another self: War-fury his name.

31

Who is the Huge One who walks over the sea, devouring the waves, who walks over the land, devouring the hills, who fears the wind but fears no man, who makes war upon the sun?

Lord, all praise, all praise, we thought it was the Fog. But it was the Dream of the Fisherman's Wife. Her eyes rolled back in the back of her head. Her legs spread wide. Her fingers went skitter-skatter across her wetness.

Everything else was pretty much just an impersonation of frost and rime. Rime itself was the mist or the fog of the frost. Bone-crunching. Iron-hard. That's how we grew to love poetry. Snatching some warmth from the vapours of death.

Mirk-flickering flame in the dawn of the north. A poet should use the expression aurora borealis once in a lifetime. And that was twice.

•

In the morning the token
The token of my presence
My presence in the rime
On blade and bough.

Life lived as heirloom.

Every event was a coin unearthed.

Fire water wind
Three mighty men

The javelin bit deep. The wolf was glad. The bow was drawn. Let's not say glad, but present.

My men reported that the wound-bees flew, and since I was light-headed to start with, I did not picture the buzzing of arrows, nor hear the humming of atoms. God grant me the maelstrom of the winds. I lost my way, like that.

From the fury of
the Northmen
deliver us,
O Lord

A furore Normannorum libera nos Domine.

V

32

I landed in this world of broken vessels.

All this eroded desolation, all this demon-ridden expanse.

All this Annihilation. The black volcanos. The ruins.
Tectonic restlessness of plates.

She had said: *I want to talk to you, at roughly four removes.*

I felt that conversation had had its day.

I had landed in this world of broken vessels. I had sensed
the emptiness as a boundless blessing.

For as long as it could, my blood would be fine.

•

And the white cockatoos came. Down the green valley,
from the opposite hill, a great flock cavorted and tumbled,
as sea-foam tumbles in a winter storm. For afternoon tea
they eat their great laments. I had been beating the night
with sticks for too long.

LUKE DAVIES

•

One becomes more completely a poet
In travelling from Babylon to Jerusalem.

(Wittgenstein)   Life is the world.

(Ace Ventura)   Pride is an abomination. One must forego the self to obtain
total spiritual creaminess, and avoid the chewy chunks
of degradation.

(Spinoza)   God is the world.

My father will be young and bold and hoist me on his
shoulders.

The world was inside me. I had become my life.

The earliest
origins of
philosophy
None of our mothers, not one of them ever, had ever died
before we were born, right back to the single cell.

Oracular virtue of the trees. Nothing but wind through
the branches.

Then I began to bear fruit. Then I began to know many
things. Then I began to thrive.

The quality of God is that he doesn't know what he's doing.
He drives on will; but at least that leaves me free, the
will-less one.

My weight is my love. My love is all my weight.

33

God has made laughter
   —I behaved myself wisely in a perfect way—
God has made laughter for me
   —I walked within my house with a perfect heart—
God has made laughter for me and all
   —I was a mighty prince among us—
God has made laughter for me and all who hear
   —For as long as it could, my blood would be fine—
God has made laughter for me and all who hear of it
   —My breath for as long as I breathed—
God has made laughter for me, and all who hear of it
   will laugh
   —Oxygen was the fabric of my exultation—
God has made laughter for me, and all who hear of it
   will laugh for me.
   —I grew, and I dwelt in the wilderness—
God has made laughter for me, and all who hear of it
   will laugh
   —I became, at last, an archer, I became an archer—

*God has made
laughter for me,
and all who hear
of it will laugh
for me.*

God has made laughter for me and all who hear of it
    —I was transformed into pure reaching—
God has made laughter for me and all who hear
    —I was the thunder, hilarity of thunder—
God has made laughter for me and all
    —I was poured out like water in the dust of death—
God has made laughter for me
    —Till the very world was flood and overflow—
God has made laughter
    —Everything present at once, as it always was—

•

God was the world, the substance of its fact, the what-is
    of his self-reckoning.

Between his self-reckoning and his improbability:
    a punchline.

•

In the secret delirium of the snows
I transengulfed the snows to prayers
I transferred prayers to the working world
Soon everyone stood transfixed & speech
Welled up in the world but I ploughed ahead
So the prayers would find their rills instead
& the rivulets left when the snowmelt came
Would be prayer-tracks set to flood again
O I came upon such emptiness
& it never stopped; no prayer was ever
Met since all was emptiness
Except that the universe is a sphere
Containing the brilliantly lit & the near
& the gods enjoyed their privileges there

•

(As for me, I abundantly uttered the memory of great
goodness.)

~

From death before we are ready to die, good Lord deliver us.

SIR FRANCIS CHICHESTER, *The Lonely Sea and the Sky*